YOUR BRAND IS YOUR BUSINESS

Your BRAND *is your* BUSINESS

JEFFREY JEROME WHITE

Briarwood Press™
PUBLISHERS

© 2025 Jeffrey White
All rights reserved.

No part of this book may be reproduced, stored in a retrieval system, or transmitted in any form or by any means—electronic, mechanical, photocopying, recording, or otherwise—without prior written permission from the publisher, except by a reviewer who may quote brief passages in a review.

Published by Briarwood Press
Memphis, Tennessee

ISBN 9798218939779

Book design by Myndshift Advertising

Printed in The United States of America

FOREWORD

When Jeffrey first spoke to me about the concept for Your Brand Is Your Business, I wasn't just struck by his professional expertise—I was moved by his heart. For years, I have watched him approach life and the world of marketing not as a game of manipulation, but as a practice of stewardship. To Jeffrey, a brand isn't a logo or a catchy slogan; it is the perception people carry about you or your business. It's the expectations they have before and after they are engaged with you, your product, or your services.

In the pages that follow, Jeffrey invites you to look past your preconceived ideals of branding and marketing. He challenges the notion that branding is just for large organizations with deep pockets. Instead, he demonstrates that the most successful and enduring brands are those who display their brand through every experience and interaction.

What I appreciate most about Your Brand Is Your Business is that it doesn't just tell you how to be seen; it teaches you how to align who you are with how you deliver. Whether you are an entrepreneur launching a new venture or a seasoned business owner looking to rediscover your "why," this book will help you tell your story and consistently demonstrate your brand.

As his pastor and friend for many years, I have seen firsthand the impact of Jeffrey's leadership. His personal brand is one of consistency, servanthood, and genuineness. He has a sincere heart to help others become a better version of themselves.

It is an honor to introduce this work, and it is my sincere hope that it provides you with the clarity and courage to build a brand that reflects the very best of who you are.

—Travis Moody

CEO, Forward Memphis

To my Lord and Savior, Jesus Christ

For your strength, patience, guidance, and direction, without which I could do nothing. It's in you that I live, move, and have my being. All glory belongs to you.

To my wife, Kathalene

My love, my partner in crime, my gift from God. Your love and support give me the freedom to do everything God has called and directed me to do. I love and appreciate you so, so much. This is just the beginning.

To my mother, Alvina Worme,
and my Grandmother (posthumously), Phyllis Jenkins

The two women who always told me I could do anything I put my mind to. There's no doubt the message you continued to drive home, gave me the confidence I needed to achieve. Thank you from the bottom of my heart.

To my father, Bennie White

The discipline you've instilled in me over the years has carried me through some of my toughest seasons. I am forever grateful for your guidance, and for the man it has helped me to become.

To my siblings—Kerry, Stephen, and Danielle

You have borne witness to the gifts given to me by God. You've not only seen them, but you've also taken part in many of their expressions over the years. While you helped me practice, those gifts were being perfected. I'm grateful to God for each of you.

Contents

Brand=Business

When most people hear the word "branding," they think of logos, colors, or taglines. But the truth is, it's far bigger than that. Branding, in the truest sense of the word, is everything your customer touches, feels, or experiences about your business. It's the way your phone is answered. How a delivery arrives. The way an employee greets, or doesn't greet, a customer. It's whether the product or service you offer does what you promised it would do. And it's how a problem is handled when something goes wrong. Your brand and your business are inseparable. They are not two different things. The moment you open your doors, answer your phone, or deliver a product, you're shaping how customers see you.

That's the part most business owners miss.

If your customer service is excellent, your brand will be known for excellence. If your delivery is sloppy, your brand will earn a reputation for being sloppy. If your message is confusing, your brand will appear confusing to everyone around you. You can spend thousands on a slick ad campaign, but if the service behind it is poor, or your product doesn't deliver on its promise, you've only sped up the rate at which people discover the truth.

Here's the simplest way to think about it.

Your brand is the promise you make. Your marketing is how you communicate that promise. Your business is how you deliver it. When those three pieces are aligned, customers trust you. And trust is the real currency of business.

This book will help you see branding not as an accessory, but as the backbone of your business. If you get your brand right, you'll find that advertising works better, word of mouth spreads faster, and loyalty grows stronger. If you get it wrong—or worse, ignore it—you'll feel like you're constantly fighting uphill just to be noticed.

In the chapters that follow, we'll reframe what branding really means, why it matters for small businesses in particular, and how you can take control of the way people perceive you. Because whether you realize it or not, customers already have a picture of your business in their minds. The only question is: are you shaping it, or letting it shape itself?

CHAPTER 1

What Brand Really Means

Ask ten business owners what a "brand" is, and most of them will give you the same answer: a logo. Maybe they'll expand it to include a color scheme or a catchy tagline. Some might even mention a website or social media presence. All of those things are important, but they are not your brand.

Your brand is not your logo. It's not your website. It's not your Instagram feed. Those are tools. They're expressions. At best, they're shorthand. But none of them, by themselves, define what your brand really is.

So what is it?

Your brand is the way people perceive your business. It's the promise you make to them, spoken or unspoken. It's what they expect before they ever hand you money, and it's what they remember afterward. Your brand is the gut-level feeling people have when they hear your name or see your product.

That means you don't get to decide whether or not you have a brand. You already have one. The moment someone interacts with your business—visits your store, calls your office, opens your email, scrolls past your ad—they're forming an opinion. They're making a judgment. And those judgments, over time, add up to your brand.

Here's where many small business owners stumble: they think branding is something separate from the daily work of running their company. They imagine it's something they'll polish up later, when they have more time or money. But the truth is, your brand is being defined right now, by every customer interaction.

Think about it this way:

- A beautifully designed ad that promises fast service doesn't matter if the person answering the phone is curt or unhelpful.
- A great-looking storefront won't save you if the inside is messy and disorganized.
- A slick logo can't cover for a product that doesn't do what it claims.

Everything your business does communicates. Whether you intend it to or not, it shapes perception. And that perception shapes your brand.

This is why brand and business can't be separated. They rise and fall together. A strong brand isn't built on clever advertising; it's built on consistency. When what you promise and what you deliver match up, people trust you. When they don't, trust breaks down, and with it, your reputation.

If you want to understand what your brand really means, stop looking at your logo for a moment. Instead, ask:

- How do customers feel after doing business with us?
- What do they tell their friends?
- Would they come back again, and would they bring someone with them?

Those answers—not the size of your ad budget—will tell you what your brand truly is.

Perception is Reality

A brand lives in the minds of your customers. It's not what you say it is; it's what they believe it is. And that belief is shaped by every experience they have with you.

This is why you can't buy your way into a strong brand with advertising alone. Ads may create awareness, but they don't guarantee trust. Trust comes when what you claim and what you deliver are the same thing.

If your service is friendly, professional, and reliable, people will feel confident about doing business with you. If your product consistently solves their problem, they'll recommend you to others. If your staff treats them with respect, they'll return, even if they could get the same product cheaper somewhere else. That's the power of brand perception, and it's built far more by what you do than what you say.

Everything Is Branding

Here's the shift every small business owner needs to make: branding is not a department, a campaign, or a line item on your budget. Branding is everything you do that affects how people experience your business.

It's the way you greet a customer at the counter. It's how quickly you respond to an email. It's the tone of voice on your website copy. It's the way your invoices look, or the condition of the box your product ships in. All of these things create an impression, and that impression is branding.

You can think of advertising as the loudspeaker for your brand; it tells the world who you are. But it's your daily actions and customer experiences that either prove or disprove the message.

The Brand Equation

To keep it simple, remember this:
- Your brand is the promise.
- Your marketing is how you demonstrate that promise.
- Your business is how you fulfill it.

When these three things line up, your brand becomes powerful. When they don't, customers notice immediately. A business that promises one thing and delivers another can spend years trying to rebuild lost trust.

Why This Matters for You

If you own a small business, you don't have the luxury of massive ad budgets or global name recognition. What you do have is control over the experience you provide. You can deliver personal attention, authenticity, and consistency in a way that big companies often struggle with. That's your advantage.

But only if you recognize that everything you do is branding. Ignore that truth, and you'll wonder why your ads don't work, why word of mouth doesn't spread, and why customers don't come back. Embrace it, and you'll start to see your brand as more than a logo on a sign—you'll see it as the living, breathing reputation that drives your entire business forward.

Closing Thought:

Your brand isn't something you build once and forget. It's something you reinforce every single day, in every interaction. It's not optional. It's not secondary. It's not waiting for a bigger budget. Your brand is happening now. So lead it with intention, or be prepared to live with the results.

CHAPTER 2

Brand=Trust

If there's one word that explains why some businesses thrive while others struggle, it's trust. Customers buy from people and companies they trust. They return to the businesses they trust. They recommend the brands they trust to friends and family. Without trust, every sale feels like starting over.

Think about the last time you recommended a business to someone. Maybe it was a restaurant, a mechanic, a lawn service, or a boutique. You didn't recommend it because of their logo. You didn't even recommend it because of their ad. You recommended it because you trusted them to deliver the same good experience to someone else that they delivered to you.

Trust is what allows businesses to grow beyond one-off sales. A slick campaign might win you a customer once, but only trust will keep them coming back. And here's the secret: people don't build trust with ads. They build trust with experiences.

Trust Comes from Consistency

When customers know what to expect from you, and you deliver on it consistently, trust grows. That's why branding is not just about the message you put out into the world. It's about whether that message matches the reality of doing business with you.

A local bakery that always has warm, fresh bread at 8 a.m. is building a brand of reliability. A handyman who shows up when he says he will is building a brand of professionalism. A boutique that remembers your name and your favorite style is building a brand of personal care. None of these things are "advertising," but all of them are branding. And all of them are how trust is earned.

On the other hand, when a business promises one thing and delivers another, trust is broken. A restaurant that advertises "fast service" but keeps customers waiting an hour isn't just slow; it's untrustworthy. And once that trust is broken, customers rarely give you a second chance.

Why Small Businesses Have an Edge

Large corporations spend billions trying to manufacture trust. They pour money into PR, advertising, sponsorships, and polished campaigns designed to convince you they care. Small businesses, on the other hand, don't need to manufacture it. They can earn it directly.

You can look a customer in the eye, deliver on your word, and follow through in a way that feels human. You can respond faster, care more deeply, and personalize the experience in ways a big company simply can't. For small businesses, trust isn't built with slogans. It's built with actions.

The Currency of Business

In many ways, trust is the real currency your business runs on. Money may change hands, but trust is what makes the money flow in the first place. Without it, transactions are fragile and short-lived. With it, transactions multiply into relationships, relationships into loyalty, and loyalty into growth.

The stronger your brand, the stronger the trust. And the stronger the trust, the stronger your business. It's a simple chain reaction.

Closing Thought:

You can outspend competitors on advertising. You can out-design them on a website. But if you can't out-deliver them on trust, none of it matters. Branding and trust are two sides of the same coin, and the businesses that understand this are the ones that stand the test of time.

CHAPTER 3

Finding Your Story

Every business has a story. The question is whether you're telling it or letting someone else fill in the blanks.

People don't connect deeply with products or services alone. They connect with meaning. They want to know why you exist, not just what you sell. That's where your brand story comes in. It gives people a reason to care, a reason to choose you over the next option, and a reason to remember you when they're deciding who to trust with their time or money.

Why Story Matters

Humans are wired for story. From the time we were drawing pictures on cave walls, we've been making sense of the world by telling and retelling narratives. A good story engages the heart before it convinces the head. And in business, that's powerful—because most buying decisions are emotional before they're rational.

When a customer hears your story and sees themselves in it, they feel a connection. They feel like they're part of something bigger than a transaction. That connection is what transforms a one-time buyer into a long-term supporter.

What Makes a Good Brand Story

A strong brand story isn't a polished slogan cooked up in a brainstorming session. It's not corporate-speak or jargon-heavy mission statements. A real story is honest, human, and easy to understand.

Your story should answer three simple questions:

1. **Why do you exist?** (What problem were you created to solve?)
2. **Who do you serve?** (Who are the people you're trying to help, and what do they care about?)
3. **How are you different?** (What makes your approach unique compared to the alternatives?)

When you can answer these in plain language, you have the foundation of a story worth telling.

Story in Action

Think about the businesses you personally admire. Chances are, you can tell their story. Maybe it's the coffee shop that opened because the owners wanted a community hub, not just another place to grab caffeine. Or the auto repair shop started by a father and daughter who believed honesty should come before upselling. Or the tech startup that was born out of one person's frustration with a problem no one else seemed to care about.

These stories do more than explain how a business began. They signal values. They create identity. They make people feel like they're choosing not just a product, but a point of view.

Your Story as a Compass

Your brand story isn't only for your customers; it's for you, too. When you know your story, you know your direction. It becomes a compass for decisions. Does this new service fit with who we are? Does this partnership make sense for our values? Are we telling a consistent story across every channel?

Without a clear story, businesses drift. They chase trends. They send mixed messages. They confuse customers, and themselves. But with a clear story, every decision becomes easier, and every piece of communication becomes more consistent.

Closing Thought:

Your story is your foundation. It's the starting point for your brand, the reason behind your promise, and the spark that makes people remember you. Don't bury it under clichés or assume people don't care. They care more than you think. If you don't tell your story, someone else will. And chances are, they won't tell it the way you want it told.

CHAPTER 4

Identity & Expression

Your story is the foundation of your brand. But a foundation on its own isn't enough—you need walls, windows, and a roof so people can actually see and experience what you've built. That's where identity and expression come in.

Identity is how your brand looks, sounds, and feels in the world. Expression is how you bring that identity to life across every touchpoint. Together, they turn your story into something customers can recognize, remember, and connect with.

More Than a Logo

A logo is important, but it isn't your brand. It's a symbol, a shortcut. It gives people a visual hook to associate with your business. But if there's nothing behind it, it's just decoration.

Think about some of the most iconic brands in the world. The golden arches of McDonald's. The swoosh of Nike. The bitten apple of Apple. Those logos are powerful because of what they represent, not just how they look. Without the reputation, consistency, and experiences tied to them, they'd be just shapes.

For a small business, the same is true. Your logo matters. But it only matters as much as the identity and experience behind it.

Voice and Tone

Identity isn't only visual; it's also verbal. How do you sound when you talk to your customers? Is your tone friendly, professional, playful, authoritative? Do you speak in plain language or industry jargon?

The way you communicate shapes how people feel about you. A warm, approachable voice makes people feel welcome. A confident, expert tone makes them feel secure. A casual, humorous style makes you feel relatable. The right voice reinforces your story and makes your brand feel human.

Bringing Identity to Life

Once you've defined your visuals and voice, the real work begins: consistency. Identity only works when it's expressed the same way across every touchpoint.

That means:

- Your website looks and sounds like your business card.
- Your social media posts match the tone of your customer emails.
- Your storefront feels like the same business people found online.

When identity and expression line up, people know what to expect. And as we've already seen, consistency builds trust.

The Risk of Mixed Signals

Nothing confuses customers faster than inconsistency. Imagine a restaurant with a polished, high-end website but sloppy menus and disorganized service. Or a professional law firm whose social media posts sound like a teenager's text messages. Or a wellness brand that preaches calm and balance but blasts its customers with aggressive, hard-sell advertising.

Mixed signals erode credibility. They make people question who you really are. And when people question you, they hesitate to buy.

Closing Thought:

Identity and expression are how your story shows up in the real world. They take your promise and give it form. They turn your values into visuals, your perspective into a voice, and your business into something people can instantly recognize. Done well, identity and expression make your brand memorable. Done poorly—or inconsistently—they make it forgettable, or worse, untrustworthy. The key is alignment. Every piece of your brand should feel like it comes from the same place, points to the same story, and delivers the same promise. That's when customers stop seeing you as "just another business" and start seeing you as the business they trust.

CHAPTER 5

Consistency Is Power

If there's one trait that separates strong brands from weak ones, it's consistency. A brand that says one thing in its advertising but delivers another in its service won't last long. Customers notice the gap immediately, and once trust is broken, it's hard to win back.

Consistency is what ties your story, identity, and expression together. It's what makes your brand recognizable and reliable. And for small businesses, it's the difference between being just another option and becoming the go-to choice.

The Promise and the Delivery

Every business makes promises, whether intentional or not. A slogan might say "fast and friendly," a website might promise "quality you can trust," or a social media ad might highlight "unbeatable prices." Those are promises.

But if the experience doesn't match, those words become empty. A promise without delivery is worse than no promise at all, because it actively damages credibility. Customers don't just walk away disappointed. They walk away doubting you.

On the other hand, when your delivery matches your promise, customers feel reassured. They know what to expect, and they feel safe putting their trust in you again and again.

Why Consistency Builds Trust

Consistency tells people: you can count on us. It reassures them that their last good experience wasn't an accident. It tells them you're not just lucky; you're reliable.

Think about your favorite local businesses. Chances are, they're the ones that deliver the same positive experience every time. The food is just as good on a Tuesday as it is on a Friday. The service is just as attentive when they're busy as when they're slow. The product quality doesn't slip, even when no one's watching.

That steadiness is what builds loyalty. Customers don't want to roll the dice every time they buy. They want to know what they're going to get. Consistency provides that certainty.

The Cost of Inconsistency

Now flip the script. Imagine a business that sometimes gets it right and sometimes doesn't. The product is great one week and sloppy the next. The service depends on who happens to be working. The message changes so often that customers aren't sure what the business really stands for.

This inconsistency is brand poison. It creates confusion. It erodes trust. It makes people hesitate to recommend you, because they can't be sure their friends will have the same experience they did.

Worse, inconsistency wastes marketing dollars. You can run the best ad campaign in the world, but if the customer's actual experience doesn't match the ad, you've just paid to accelerate disappointment.

Consistency Across Touchpoints

Consistency doesn't just apply to customer service or product quality. It applies everywhere your brand shows up.

- Online and offline: Your website should match the feel of your store or office.
- Marketing and reality: Ads should reflect the true experience, not an exaggerated version of it.
- Team behavior: Every employee should deliver the same level of professionalism, not just the "good ones."

When all of these touchpoints line up, your brand feels whole. Customers sense that alignment, even if they can't articulate it. And it gives them confidence to keep coming back.

Closing Thought:

Consistency isn't glamorous. It doesn't always grab headlines. But it's what separates brands that flare up for a moment from those that endure for years. When your promise and delivery are aligned—every day, across every touchpoint—you become more than a business. You become a trusted part of people's lives. And in the long run, trust beats clever marketing every time.

CHAPTER 6

The Small Business Advantage

When most small business owners think about branding, they feel at a disadvantage. They imagine the massive budgets of national chains, the polished campaigns of global corporations, and the kind of name recognition that only comes from years of saturation. It's easy to think, how could we ever compete with that?

But here's the truth: small businesses have advantages big companies would pay fortunes to reclaim. You may not have their money, but you have something just as powerful: authenticity, agility, and personal connection. And if you lean into those strengths, you can build a brand that feels more human, more memorable, and more trustworthy than any big-box competitor.

Authenticity Over Gloss

Customers know when they're being sold to. They know when a campaign is overproduced, when a message has been crafted by a committee, and when a company is saying something just because it sounds good. Big corporations often fall into this trap. They polish their message so much that it loses its humanity.

Small businesses, on the other hand, can be real. They can tell their story honestly. They can show the people behind the work. They can connect with customers in a way that feels genuine, not scripted.

Authenticity builds trust, and trust builds loyalty. When your customers believe you mean what you say—and see you follow through—they'll stand by you even when cheaper or flashier options are available.

Agility as a Weapon

Large companies move slowly. Every decision has to pass through layers of approval. Campaigns take months to launch. By the time they act, the opportunity may already be gone.

Small businesses can turn on a dime. You can adapt quickly to new trends, respond directly to customer feedback, and experiment without getting stuck in red tape. If something's not working, you can change it tomorrow. If a new opportunity pops up, you can seize it immediately.

That agility is part of your brand. It tells customers you're alive, responsive, and attentive to what's happening right now, not just running on autopilot.

Personal Connection

Here's the advantage money can't buy: relationships. A small business owner can know their customers by name. They can remember preferences. They can create moments of connection that feel impossible in a giant corporation.

That personal connection is one of the most powerful forms of branding there is. When people feel seen and valued, they become not just customers, but advocates. They'll recommend you to others. They'll defend you when competitors try to lure them away. They'll stay loyal because they feel like they're part of your story.

Competing on Strengths, Not Scale

You don't need to compete with big brands on their terms. You don't need the biggest ad spend or the flashiest campaign. What you need is consistency, authenticity, and a story that resonates.

The truth is, customers don't always want the biggest name; they want the best experience. And small businesses can deliver that in ways the giants can't.

Closing Thought:

Your advantage isn't in trying to look bigger than you are. It's in being exactly what you are: small enough to care, quick enough to adapt, and human enough to connect. When you embrace those strengths, your brand becomes more than a logo, more than a tagline, more than a campaign. It becomes a living promise that no competitor can easily copy.

CHAPTER 7

Pitfalls To Avoid

Building a brand doesn't have to be complicated, but it does require awareness. Many small businesses stumble not because they lack passion or skill, but because they fall into common traps. These pitfalls are easy to slip into, but the good news is they're just as easy to avoid once you know what to look for.

Mistaking a Logo for a Brand

One of the biggest misconceptions is equating "brand" with "logo." A logo is important, yes—it's a symbol customers can instantly recognize. But if you treat it as your brand, you'll miss the bigger picture.

A logo without a clear story, consistent service, and meaningful experiences behind it is just a graphic. It won't win loyalty on its own. Too many businesses believe that once they've "gotten the logo done," their branding work is finished. In reality, that's only the beginning.

Inconsistency

Inconsistency is one of the fastest ways to erode trust. When your ads say one thing but your service delivers another, people notice. When your tone on social media doesn't match the experience customers have in person, they notice that too.

Every mismatch, no matter how small, creates doubt. And doubt makes customers hesitate. It's far better to deliver a simple, consistent brand than a flashy but uneven one.

Great Ads, Poor Experience

Here's a trap many businesses fall into: investing heavily in advertising while neglecting the basics of customer experience. A clever ad might get people in the door, but if what they find doesn't live up to the promise, the ad does more harm than good.

Marketing can amplify a truth, but it can't disguise a lie. If your service is poor, no campaign in the world can fix it. At best, it will only speed up the rate at which people discover the problem.

Chasing Trends

It's tempting to copy whatever's popular in the moment: a new social media style, a catchy phrase, a trendy design. But trends fade, and when they do, businesses built on them fade too.

This doesn't mean you should ignore cultural shifts or refuse to evolve. It means you should filter every new trend through your brand story. Does it fit who you are? Does it reinforce your values? If not, resist the urge to chase it. Your brand should be timeless, not disposable.

Trying to Be Everything to Everyone

Another pitfall is spreading yourself too thin. In an effort to appeal to everyone, many businesses dilute their message until it means nothing to anyone. Strong brands are clear about who they serve and what they stand for.

When you try to be everything, you risk being forgettable. When you focus, you become memorable. Customers are drawn to businesses with a clear identity. Even if that means not everyone is your customer.

Closing Thought:

Avoiding these pitfalls isn't about perfection. It's about awareness. The goal isn't to never make mistakes. It's to build a brand strong enough that customers know what you stand for, even if you stumble now and then. If you can keep your focus on delivering consistently, telling your story honestly, and resisting the urge to chase every shiny object, you'll avoid the most common traps that sink small business branding.

CHAPTER 8

Real-World Branding In Action

Branding doesn't live in theory; it's built in practice. It shows up in the choices businesses make every day—in how they communicate, deliver, and show up for their customers. The following examples highlight small businesses that turned clarity, consistency, and story into measurable growth. Each one demonstrates that when identity, message, and experience work together, branding stops being an idea and becomes a true business advantage.

Crafting a Brand Built On Mastery

ProFix Handyman Solutions is a great example of what happens when a strong reputation isn't matched by a strong brand.

Tommy Childress had all the ingredients for trust: craftsmanship, consistency, and a level of detail that reminded us of the masters he naturally works like. Artists such as Da Vinci, Michelangelo, Chagall, Monet, and Picasso. But his identity didn't communicate any of that. The perception lagged behind the reality.

When we rebranded ProFix, we built the system around the same principles that guided those masters: precision, proportion, restraint, and respect for materials. We didn't imitate their aesthetics. We adopted their discipline. The typography, colors, spacing, and imagery were designed to reflect the intentionality behind Tommy's work.

The result? His brand finally caught up with his reputation. Engagement increased, referrals strengthened, and high-value project inquiries rose because the identity now signaled the level of mastery people were already experiencing.

Branding didn't invent craftsmanship. But it made the truth unmistakable.

The result proved a simple truth: when a brand reflects its values with consistency and craft, reputation becomes its strongest marketing.

Building a Brand Around Belonging

901FitLife launched with a bold mission: to create a safe, welcoming space for women—especially those new to fitness—to feel empowered and motivated in their wellness journey. Founder Lisa Monger wanted the brand to represent more than workouts; she wanted it to embody encouragement, empathy, and emotional wellness.

With creative partnership from Myndshift, the brand came to life through a multi-platform strategy that blended authenticity and aspiration. Every element—from the empowering tone of its messaging to the community-driven campaign design—reinforced one idea: fitness is not just physical, it's emotional.

The impact reached beyond brand buzz. 901FitLife became known as a place where women felt seen, supported, and inspired to grow, both inside and out.

It was proof that when a brand's message aligns with its mission, customers are more likely to become an engaged community.

Driving Desire Through Experience

Dream Rentals, Memphis' first luxury vehicle rental service, made a striking debut. Word of mouth was strong, the clientele impressed, and the cars—sleek, high-end, aspirational—spoke for themselves. But one year after launch, momentum began to slow. The brand needed to evolve from novelty to necessity, building staying power in a market where new competitors were gaining ground.

Myndshift refined the in-store experience with bold, high-end visuals that matched the sophistication of the fleet. The team then expanded outward with a print and outdoor campaign supported by geo-fenced digital ads targeting luxury car shoppers and travelers near the showroom. The result was a seamless, multi-touch experience that surrounded the customer with the brand at every point of contact.

Within a week of launch, showroom traffic jumped 36%. Luxury SUV and premium sedan rentals climbed more than 28% during the same period. Dream Rentals didn't just regain momentum. It redefined what premium service meant in its category.

The campaign showed that when brand and experience move in sync, awareness doesn't just grow; it gains momentum.

Elevating Innovation Through Design

When broker Neil Hubbard—renowned for representing some of Memphis' most luxurious properties—was selected to market the city's first zero-carbon, zero-energy home, he turned to Myndshift to match the innovation of the listing with branding worthy of its breakthrough.

Myndshift developed a refined brochure and visual system that blended sustainability with sophistication, mirroring the home's fusion of modern technology and timeless design. Every detail, from typography to texture, was crafted to communicate quiet luxury and forward-thinking elegance.

The collateral didn't just market a property; it positioned Civitas as a brand that redefines what "luxury living" can mean in an environmentally conscious world.

This proved that when story and design work together, innovation can really shine.

The Common Thread

What do these stories have in common? Each business discovered that branding wasn't just about design or advertising; it was about aligning who they were with how they delivered. They found their story, expressed it consistently, and lived it out through every interaction.

None of them had the biggest budgets or the fanciest campaigns. But by focusing on what mattered most—trust, story, and experience—they created brands that stood out in their own markets.

Closing Thought:

Branding doesn't require a Madison Avenue budget. It requires clarity, consistency, and courage. When you lean into what makes your business unique and deliver on it faithfully, you create something no competitor can copy: trust.

CHAPTER 9

From Brand To Business Growth

Strong branding isn't just about looking good. It's not even just about being remembered. At its core, branding is about creating the conditions for growth. When customers know who you are, what you stand for, and what they can expect from you, growth becomes a natural byproduct.

Branding as an Investment, Not an Expense

Many small business owners look at branding as a cost, something they'll get to once sales pick up. But the reality is the opposite: strong branding makes sales easier, marketing more effective, and customers more loyal. It's not an expense; it's an investment that pays dividends over time.

Consider two businesses offering the same service at the same price. One has no clear identity, inconsistent service, and a forgettable message. The other has a recognizable look, a clear promise, and consistent delivery. Which one do you think wins more customers? Which one commands higher trust? Which one gets recommended more often?

That's the power of branding. It multiplies the impact of everything else you do.

The Pricing Advantage

A trusted brand can charge more. Customers aren't just buying the product or service; they're buying confidence, peace of mind, and reliability.

That's why people will pay more for the same cup of coffee at a café they love, or spend extra on a contractor they believe will get the job done right the first time.

Branding gives you permission to compete on value instead of price. And once you stop competing solely on price, you open the door to healthier margins and sustainable growth.

The Loyalty Loop

Acquiring a customer is hard. Keeping one is easier, if you've built trust. When people trust your brand, they don't just buy once; they come back. They also spread the word, becoming advocates who do your marketing for you.

This "loyalty loop" is one of the most valuable assets a small business can build. Instead of spending all your energy chasing new customers, your existing ones bring others along. Word of mouth is still the most powerful form of advertising, and it's free.

Growth Beyond Marketing

A strong brand doesn't just grow your sales. It grows your opportunities. It attracts better partnerships. It draws in stronger employees. It makes investors or lenders more willing to believe in your future. In short, it opens doors that a weak or inconsistent brand will never reach.

Think about it: would you rather partner with a business that feels scattered, or one that looks and acts like it has its act together? Would you rather work for a company that seems uncertain about its identity, or one that clearly knows who it is and where it's going?

That's the ripple effect of branding. It strengthens every aspect of the business, not just the bottom line.

Closing Thought:

Growth doesn't come from luck. It comes from clarity, consistency, and trust. When your brand is strong, customers believe in you, partners want to work with you, and employees feel proud to represent you. Your brand is the engine that powers your business forward. The stronger you build it, the faster and farther your business can go.

CHAPTER 10

The Action Plan

By now, you've seen that branding isn't a side project. It's not just a logo, a website, or a clever tagline. Your brand is your business. And your business is your brand. The question is, how do you put that knowledge into practice?

This chapter is designed to give you practical steps you can take right now. Think of it as a brand health check, a way to look at your business through your customers' eyes and strengthen the areas that matter most.

Step 1: Clarify Your Story

Start by writing down the answers to three simple questions:

1. Why do you exist?
2. Who do you serve?
3. How are you different?

Don't overthink it, and don't hide behind jargon. Keep it human and simple. This is the story your customers need to hear, and it should guide everything else you do.

Step 2: Define Your Promise

Every brand makes a promise, whether it's spoken or implied. Define yours clearly. What do you want people to expect from you every single time? Fast service? Personal attention? High quality? Reliability? Once you name it, you can begin delivering it with consistency.

Step 3: Audit the Experience

Walk through your business like a customer. From the first impression to the last, what do people see, hear, and feel?

- How is the phone answered?
- How does your website make people feel?
- What's the condition of your packaging, store, or office?
- How do you handle questions, problems, or complaints?

Every touchpoint is branding. Ask yourself: does this align with the promise we've made? If not, fix it.

Step 4: Align Identity and Expression

Check your visuals and voice. Do they match your story? Do they match the experience you want customers to have? Consistency here builds recognition and trust. Update anything that feels off-brand or confusing.

Step 5: Commit to Consistency

Choose the things that matter most and deliver them every single time. It's better to keep one simple promise faithfully than to make ten promises you can't keep. Reliability beats flash.

Step 6: Build for Loyalty

Think beyond the first sale. How can you make people want to come back? How can you make them want to tell others about you? Loyalty doesn't happen by accident; it happens when customers feel valued, heard, and cared for.

Step 7: Keep It Human

At the end of the day, branding is about people. Customers don't remember you for your graphics or clever headlines as much as they remember how you made them feel. Stay authentic, stay human, and don't lose sight of the relationships that drive your business.

Closing Thought:

The steps in this chapter aren't complicated, but they require discipline. They require you to care about the details, to pay attention to the customer's perspective, and to commit to living your brand every day. The good news? You don't need a massive budget to do this. You don't need to be a global giant. You just need clarity, consistency, and the courage to act on them. Your brand is happening right now, whether you manage it or not. This action plan gives you the tools to take control—so your business isn't just another name, but a brand people trust, remember, and recommend.

APPENDIX A

DIAGNOSE YOUR BRAND'S HEALTH

	YES	NO	NEEDS WORK
STORY	☐	☐	☐
PROMISE	☐	☐	☐
EXPERIENCE	☐	☐	☐
CONSISTENCY	☐	☐	☐
TRUST	☐	☐	☐
LOYALTY	☐	☐	☐
HUMANITY	☐	☐	☐

*If you can answer **yes** to most of these, your brand is in good health. If you find yourself hesitating or saying "not really," that's a sign to focus on that area before it turns into a bigger issue.*

APPENDIX B
BRAND AUDIT IN ONE PAGE

Target Audience	Positioning
Competitors	Differentiators
Brand Personality	Brand Voice
Messaging	Visual Identity

Closing Thought: *A brand audit isn't about perfection—it's about alignment. The closer your marketing, customer experience, and reputation align, the stronger your brand becomes.*

APPENDIX C
BRAND CLARITY WORKSHEETS
WORKSHEET 1
CLARIFY YOUR STORY

1. Why do we exist?
(What problem are we here to solve? What motivated us to start?)

____

____

2. Why do we serve?
(Describe your customers. What do they care about? What do they need from you?)

____

____

3. How are we different?
(What makes our approach, values, or delivery unique compared to the alternatives?)

____

____

When you can answer these clearly, you have the foundation of your brand story.

APPENDIX C
BRAND CLARITY WORKSHEETS
WORKSHEET 2
DEFINE YOUR PROMISE

"Our customers can always count on us to ________________________

____

____."

Examples:

- "Deliver projects on time—every time."
- "Make healthy eating simple and affordable."
- "Treat every customer like family."

This should be the heartbeat of your brand. If you can't keep this promise, don't make it.

APPENDIX C
BRAND CLARITY WORKSHEETS
WORKSHEET 3
THE CONSISTENCY MAP

List your main customer touchpoints. For each, note whether it feels **on-brand** (yes), **off-brand** (no), **or needs improvement** (maybe).

Touchpoint	On-Brand?	Notes
Website	Yes / No / Maybe	
Storefront / Office	Yes / No / Maybe	
Customer Service	Yes / No / Maybe	
Invoice / Receipts	Yes / No / Maybe	
Packaging	Yes / No / Maybe	
Social Media	Yes / No / Maybe	
Advertising	Yes / No / Maybe	
Follow-up / Loyalty Programs	Yes / No / Maybe	

*Use this map to spot gaps. Anywhere you see "**no**" or "**maybe**," make a plan to bring that touchpoint back in line with your promise and story.*

APPENDIX D
RESOURCES & INSPIRATION

No single book has all the answers, but some resources can sharpen your perspective and give you fresh tools. Here's a short list of books and references I recommend for small business owners who want to dive deeper into branding, marketing, and customer experience.

BOOKS

Building a StoryBrand *by Donald Miller*
A practical guide to clarifying your message so customers listen. Great for small businesses who struggle to explain what they do in a way people actually care about.

This Is Marketing *by Seth Godin*
A reminder that marketing isn't about hype—it's about solving problems, building trust, and showing up for the right people.

The Brand Gap *by Marty Neumeier*
A short but powerful book that explains the difference between business strategy and brand strategy—and why the two need to work together.

Contagious: How to Build Word of Mouth in the Digital Age *by Jonah Berger*
Explains why people share certain ideas and brands, and how you can design your message so it spreads naturally.

Delivering Happiness *by Tony Hsieh*
Part memoir, part business guide. The late Zappos founder shows how putting customer experience first can create loyalty (and profits) that last.

ONLINE RESOURCES

Harvard Business Review & Other Articles
Harvard Business Review has countless accessible articles on branding, leadership, and small business strategy. Even reading one a month can broaden your perspective and keep you inspired.

Closing the Appendices: Remember, these resources are meant to supplement—not replace—what you've built here. Your most powerful branding lessons will come from your own business: listening to customers, testing ideas, and learning what makes your brand resonate.

ACKNOWLEDGMENTS

Writing this book reminded me of something I've always believed: no brand, and no business, succeeds alone.

To the clients and small business owners who have trusted me over the years, you've been the true teachers. Every challenge, every campaign, every late-night brainstorm has shaped the lessons in these pages.

Special thanks to the collaborators and creatives who continue to raise the bar alongside me—especially the team at Myndshift, whose energy and ideas make every project stronger.

I'm also grateful to Travis Moody, CEO of Forward Memphis, for writing the foreword to this book, and for his commitment to advancing financial stability for individuals and organizations—a mission that continues to inspire my own work.

Finally, to every entrepreneur, founder, and dreamer building something of their own—this book is for you. May it remind you that your brand isn't just what you sell; it's how you show up.

FURTHER READING

If this book helped you rethink how brand and business connect, here are a few more resources that expand on the ideas within Your Brand Is Your Business.

BOOKS

- **Obviously Awesome** *by April Dunford*—A clear, practical guide to positioning your offer so customers understand its value instantly.

- **The Mom Test** *by Rob Fitzpatrick*—A sharp reminder that the best marketing insights come from listening to customers, not guessing.

- **Win Without Pitching Manifesto** *by Blair Enns*—A powerful framework for positioning service businesses as experts rather than vendors.

- **Good Strategy Bad Strategy** *by Richard Rumelt*—A concise look at what real strategy looks like—and why clarity is its foundation.

- **Play Bigger** *by Al Ramadan, Dave Peterson, Christopher Lockhead & Kevin Maney*—A strategic look at category design and why winning brands don't just compete; they define the space they play in.

ARTICLES & ONLINE RESOURCES

- **Strategyzer Insights**—Practical articles and tools on positioning, value propositions, and building businesses customers understand immediately. **strategyzer.com**

- **First Round Review**—Deep, experience-driven essays from founders and operators on messaging, positioning, and company growth. **review.firstround.com**

ABOUT THE AUTHOR

Jeffrey White is a Creative Director, Writer, and Founder of Myndshift, an independent creative agency based in Memphis, Tennessee. For more than two decades, he has helped entrepreneurs, small business owners, and growing companies clarify their message, strengthen their identity, and connect more authentically with customers—drawing inspiration from art, culture, and the everyday stories of people building something from nothing.

When he's not developing campaigns, writing his next book, mentoring, or antiquing, Jeffrey enjoys traveling and exploring local restaurants and coffee shops with his wife, Kathalene.

www.ingramcontent.com/pod-product-compliance
Lightning Source LLC
Chambersburg PA
CBHW031511150726
47990CB00007B/2965